THE

GUIDE TO MOTORING AND THE LAW

Fenton Bresler, a practising barrister since 1951, has been writing and broadcasting about the law for some 40 years. He was legal correspondent for the *Daily Mail* and *Sunday Express*, and now contributes both a weekly and monthly column to the *Daily Telegraph*. The author of more than a dozen books on crime and the law, he regularly appears on television and radio as a legal expert.

THE

DUCKHAMS

GUIDE TO MOTORING AND THE LAW

BY FENTON BRESLER

GOOD BOOKS

PRODUCED FOR DUCKHAMS OILS LIMITED
BY GOOD BOOKS (GB PUBLICATIONS LIMITED)
LAGARD FARM, WHITLEY, WILTS SN12 8RL

A CATALOGUE RECORD OF THIS BOOK
IS AVAILABLE FROM THE BRITISH LIBRARY

ISBN 0 946555 44 3

COVER DESIGN: SUMMERFIELD WILMOT KEENE
INSIDE DESIGN: DESIGN/SECTION, FROME
PRINTED AND BOUND IN GREAT BRITAIN
BY CALEDONIAN INTERNATIONAL BOOK
MANUFACTURING LTD, GLASGOW

THE AUTHOR, THE PUBLISHER, AND DUCKHAMS OILS
WOULD LIKE TO POINT OUT THAT BY ITS VERY
NATURE, LAW IS CONTINUALLY EVOLVING.
ACCORDINGLY, WHILE EVERY CARE HAS BEEN MADE
TO ENSURE THAT THE INFORMATION IS ACCURATE AT
THE DATE OF PUBLICATION, IT SHOULD NOT BE
ACTED UPON AS AN ALTERNATIVE TO LEGAL ADVICE
AND NEITHER THE AUTHOR, THE PUBLISHER NOR
DUCKHAMS OILS CAN ACCEPT RESPONSIBILITY FOR
ANY INFORMATION SET OUT IN THIS BOOK.

DUCKHAMS OILS
DUCKHAMS HOUSE
157/159 MASONS HILL
BROMLEY
KENT BR2 9HU

CONTENTS

DUCKHAMS : THE OIL SPECIALISTS

In 1899, a brilliant young chemist named Alexander Duckham began to do pioneering work into the development of lubricants for the recently invented motor car. Today, nearly 100 years on, the company he founded still stands for innovation and excellence, the Duckhams brand name a symbol of quality the world over.

No other oil company has been more successful than Duckhams in creating new products for the motorist. In the early Fifties the company launched Europe's first multigrade oil, soon to be followed by Duckhams Q, the world's first 20W/50 oil. The latter dominated the British lubricants market for the next two decades, and is still in great demand in many countries around the world.

It was during this period, in 1966, that Duckhams renewed its long association with motorsport, embracing all categories from motor cycling and saloon cars right up to Formula One. Unlike other companies, however, Duckhams declined to develop special products for competition, choosing instead to use its standard motor oil.

It was a brave decision but one that was entirely vindicated by results. More than that, the knowledge gained from the racing circuits was fed back into the development of even finer products for the consumer market.

To the amazement of some sceptics, Duckhams Q 20/50 motor oil was successfully used in Formula One racing cars, first by the Surtees team and then by Colin Chapman in the legendary Lotus — helping to bring the latter victory in the 1973 French Grand Prix. James Hunt, driving for the Hesketh team, also used Duckhams oil in winning the Dutch Grand Prix a year later.

Since the Seventies, Duckhams have focused their attention on the grass roots level of the sport, lubricating the cars and careers of many young drivers. In Formula Ford, for example, they have worked with the young Ayrton Senna, Nigel Mansell, David Coulthard and Mark Blundell. The company's latest motorsport venture is Team Mondeo, partnering Ford in their campaign to win the 1997 British Touring Car Championship.

A new age in engine technology has seen the development of turbochargers, catalysts and multivalve engines. Often leading the field with these developments, Duckhams have introduced a range of oils designed to meet the performance requirements of every type of engine.

For close to a century, Duckhams motor oils have enhanced the performance of vehicles on the road. Now we hope this book will enhance motorists' understanding of our motoring laws.

INTRODUCTION

Most of the 31.7 million qualified drivers in this country know very little about motoring law. They probably took their driving test years ago and, even if they knew the law fairly well at that time, they are unlikely to have updated themselves, except by chance from what they read or see in the media. Similarly many of the 4.7 provisional licence holders who have not yet taken their test often cannot see the wood for the trees. There simply is so much law!

Yet whether driving for a long time or still a learner, we can all benefit from guidance when dealing with the sometimes bewildering complexities of the law. Back in the Fifties, Lord Goddard, when Lord Chief Justice, calculated that there were over 1,000 offences that a driver could commit. Nowadays, the figure could probably be trebled.

Motorists come more often into contact — and, all too often, conflict — with the law than any other section of the community. They end up involved with the police and the courts more than any other normally law-abiding citizen and it is more likely to cost them hard-earned money, either by way of a fine or fixed penalty, or by paying for other methods of transport if they lose their licence through, for instance, drink-driving or a bad case of speeding.

This book will help keep you out of avoidable trouble with the law and tell you what your rights are, should you fall foul of it. It is primarily concerned with car drivers; but most of the following pages are also relevant for drivers of other motor vehicles and motorcycles.

Although it is not possible to cover everything in a book of this size, you will find most of what you need for everyday purposes. This is a guide, not a legal textbook. But all knowledge is power, and this is nowhere more true than with motoring law.

Scotland has its own legal system but, except that the names of the courts are different, this part of the law is much the same as in the rest of the United Kingdom.

Motoring law in Northern Ireland is substantially the same as elsewhere in the UK, but there are important differences — for example, the system of penalty points, though planned, has not yet come into force in the province — so motorists there should make a point of checking that the information in this guide applies locally.

Fenton Bresler
January, 1997

GETTING STARTED

Taking the Driving Test

You cannot legally drive without passing it and recently it has been made even more difficult. As from 1 July 1996, the Driving Test has been divided into two parts. There is now a written theory test which everyone must pass before being allowed to take the old practical test, sitting alone at the wheel under an examiner's vigilant eye.

You must, of course, first learn to drive. The basic minimum requirements are that learners must be at least 17, hold a provisional licence (obtainable for £21 at a post office), display on the back and front of the vehicle L-plates specified in the 1987 Motor Vehicles (Driving Licence) Regulations (a red letter "L", 102mm high by 89mm wide by 38mm thick, on a white card 178mm square) — and not drive on motorways. The learner must also be accompanied by someone of at least 21 who has held a full British licence for that type of car for at least three years.

But there is more to it than that.

Professional instructors who teach learners for payment must be approved by the Driving Standards Agency, an Executive Agency of the Department of

Transport, register with that agency and display their approval certificate on the tuition car's windscreen. But even non-professionals cannot simply sit back and enjoy the scenery. They must supervise the driving of the novice at the wheel.

If not, they can *both* find themselves in legal trouble. Back in 1940, in a case where the "supervising" driver had failed to warn a learner not to overtake before a dangerous bend and he had crashed into an oncoming lorry, a High Court judge upheld the learner's conviction of careless driving *and* his companion's conviction of aiding and abetting.

He ruled: "It is the supervisor's duty, when necessary, to do whatever can reasonably be expected to prevent the driver from acting unskilfully or carelessly or in a manner likely to cause danger to others."

That still remains the law, for all motoring offences. Technically, the supervising driver may even be guilty of aiding and abetting — and, therefore, also liable to be fined — when a learner commits a simple parking offence.

Similar considerations apply if the learner has an accident and the victim sues him for damages. As Lord Denning once said: "It is no answer to say, 'I was a learner driver under instruction. I was doing my best and could not help it.' The law requires the same standard of care as from any other driver. He may be doing his best but his incompetent best is not good enough."

This ruling has two by-products:

(i) The learner — or his insurance company — may even have to pay damages to his own accompanying driver, if reasonable supervision could not have prevented the accident. But the supervisor would have to prove — and this is most important — that he had not accepted the risk of uncompensated injury by, for instance, checking beforehand with the learner that he was insured.

(ii) If, however, the accident could have been avoided by reasonable supervision (grabbing the wheel or handbrake, even just shouting), the so-called supervisor will have to share in any damages paid to an injured third party, and damages for his own injuries would be cut because of his own "contributory negligence".

I will shortly deal with insurance generally but there is one other vitally important point for learners, and for any qualified driver allowing a learner to drive his car. That driving will *not* be covered by insurance unless the car owner has previously told his insurance company. They must be given an opportunity to charge an increased premium because there is a learner at the wheel.

Many people do not always realise what they are taking on when helping a relative or friend to learn to drive.

Driving Licence

An essential document. On passing your driving test, you will simply exchange your provisional licence — at no extra charge — for a full one, *which you must promptly sign*. But, of course, the licence will only entitle you to drive the type of vehicle for which you have passed the test. If you have passed with an automatic car, you will not be allowed to drive a manual one. However, passing on a manual will allow you to drive an automatic.

A full licence usually lasts until you are 70, when you can go on renewing it indefinitely for three years at a time at a cost (at the moment) of £6.

There is no legal age at which you must hand in your licence. So long as you keep a reasonably clean record, it is entirely up to you when you decide because of increasing age to stop driving: my mother-in-law carried on until she was 91, although she had the good sense not to drive on very busy roads.

There are only two ways to lose your licence against your will. The first is if a court disqualifies you. This will be for a fixed period which, depending on the offence, can be for anything from several weeks or months to, in theory, life. In practice, 20 years is the longest likely disqualification — for a persistently bad driver with a truly appalling record.

The second way to lose your licence is to develop a major medical or physical disability which, in the terms of the 1988 Road Traffic Act, makes your driving a source of danger to the public. You must then inform the Driver and Vehicle Licensing Centre (DVLC) at Swansea which may revoke your licence, but in some cases you can appeal to a magistrates' court.

Section 163 of the 1988 Act gives a uniformed police officer the right to stop you at any time when you are driving and ask for your licence. If you do not produce it to him or at a police station of your choice within seven days, or "as soon as reasonably practicable" thereafter, you commit an offence for which you can be fined up to £1,000. Driving without having a licence at all is, of course, much more serious. You can be fined up to £1,000, have three to six penalty points endorsed on any licence that you may obtain in future and even, in a really bad case, be disqualified — unless, that is, you can persuade the police to offer you a fixed penalty.

Explaining Vital Terms

Notice those vital expressions in the last paragraph: fined up to £1,000, licence endorsed, penalty points and fixed penalty. You are continually going to come across them in this book and they are essential to an understanding of modern motoring law; yet many motorists have only a hazy idea of their meaning. So let us explain them at this early stage.

Fined up to £1,000

All motoring offences carry maximum fines which can be £1,000, £2,500 or £5,000. These are the amounts "up to" which a court can impose a fine. They are Parliament's way of showing its view of the seriousness of that type of offence, but the actual amount in any particular case will depend on its own specific facts and will generally be much less, especially with a first or infrequent offender.

Licence endorsed

If you are convicted of anything except the most minor offence, the 1988 Road Traffic Offenders Act says that the court must order the facts of the conviction and sentence to be endorsed — ie written — on your licence. The idea is to create an instantly available record so that any police officer, or magistrate, looking at your licence in the future can immediately see your legal track record.

But a court can decide not to endorse (and even, with a major offence, not to disqualify, or to do so for a lesser period) if you can persuade it that "special reasons" exist.

You will have to attend court and give evidence and, as we shall see later, probably engage a lawyer to speak for you, even if pleading guilty. It is usually an uphill task. As the High Court ruled 50 years ago, "the reasons must be special to the offence and not to the offender".

You cannot argue that your own personal circumstances are "special": for instance, that you would lose your job if your licence were endorsed or you were disqualified. Tough! There must be something special about the circumstances of the actual offence: for instance, you were speeding your heavily pregnant wife to hospital in an emergency when no other transport was available.

Penalty points

When an offence is sufficiently major to warrant a licence being endorsed, the court will usually also impose "penalty points". These are valid for three years, although after four years (11 years with drink-driving) you can send your licence to the DVLC at Swansea and ask them to reissue it with the points deleted; which is always worth doing. It can be psychologically useful to show a police officer, if stopped, a beautifully clean licence.

Acquiring too many penalty points can lead to disqualification. This is called "Totting-up". If you commit an endorsable offence which "tots up" to 12 the points incurred over the past three years up to your latest offence, a court *must* disqualify you for at least six months. If you commit more than one offence at the same time (for example, passing a red traffic light and speeding while having defective tyres), although each offence carries its own number of points, only the most points attached to any one offence will be counted.

Points can easily mount up over three years with a none-too-careful driver and he can only avoid a minimum six months' disqualification if the court accepts there are "grounds for mitigating the normal consequences of the conviction".

This is easier to establish than "special reasons". You *can* plead your personal circumstances: for instance, that you would lose your job if disqualified or an innocent person would suffer, such as an elderly relative dependent on you for transport — but of late the courts have toughened their stance.

How many points are likely in any particular case? It varies. Less serious offences (defective tyres, failing to comply with traffic lights, etc) carry their own fixed number, usually three. But more serious offences have a range where a court can select how many it considers appropriate. Examples are: speeding — three to six points; careless driving — three to nine points; failing to stop or report after an accident — five to ten points.

Fixed Penalty

This system exists to ease the log-jam in the courts and encourage the motorist to accept his guilt by offering him the soft option of a fixed penalty. The court system is bypassed and you pay to the local Fixed Penalty Office a £20 penalty for a non-endorsable offence, such as seat belt or lighting offences. Or a £40 penalty for endorsable offences, such as speeding, defective tyres or failing to comply with traffic lights. Furthermore, if the offence carries penalty points, the Fixed Penalty Office will only order three penalty points to be endorsed on your licence.

This really is a good deal. You are guaranteed these fixed penalties and fixed points, although (certainly) the fine and (perhaps) the number of points would be more if you took the case to court.

Fixed penalties are not available for the most serious offences, such as careless or dangerous driving or drink-driving, but they cover a wide spectrum of medium-scale offences. In penalty point cases, only a uniformed police officer can hand you a fixed penalty notice, and he will only do so if you surrender your driving licence on the spot or within seven days at a police station of your choice and he sees that you are not liable for "totting-up". It also helps to be polite!

If the offence does not carry penalty points, a uniformed police officer or traffic warden can leave the fixed penalty notice attached to your vehicle, usually stuck on your windscreen. This most often happens in parking cases, except in London, Winchester and Oxford where a different system prevails.

Unless you really have a burning sense of injustice, you should accept the offer contained in a fixed penalty notice. It will almost certainly cost less than if you went to court, even if you are innocent. That is the grim reality of motoring law today.

Insurance

Section 143 of the 1988 Road Traffic Act makes it a serious offence to use a car on a road without insurance. It lays down a maximum £5,000 fine, endorsement with six to eight points, discretionary disqualification — and the fixed penalty system does not apply.

Furthermore, "using" a car means more than merely driving it. You "use" your car, even if you merely have it parked on the road outside your house with no immediate intention of driving it. Provided it is still capable of being driven, and so comes within the legal definition of a "motor vehicle", you breach Section 143 if, for instance, you have let its insurance lapse.

All policies must be read carefully for their own detailed cover, including whether it is limited only to a "named driver" or to *any* qualified driver; but three main types of motor insurance are available:

Third Party Only is the legal minimum cover, and the cheapest. If you have an accident wholly or even partly your fault, your insurance company will pay for damage to the vehicle or property of, or bodily injury to, anyone else involved (ie the "third party") — which can include your own passenger.

But you will have to pay for repairing or replacing your own car and, if the third party were to blame, your insurers will not help you pursue your claim against them. It is nothing to do with them.

Third Party Fire and Theft is one step more than the minimum. It will also cover you against your own car being stolen or damaged in a fire. But no more.

Comprehensive is the most expensive form of cover and goes well beyond the legal minimum. It will not only cover you against damage or bodily injury to "third parties" but also loss of, or damage to, your own car up to its insured value.

But, and I only discovered this the hard way after an accident which was not my fault and in which I was nearly killed, it will only cover you against the death or bodily injury of yourself or your spouse travelling with you *up to an amount stated in the policy*, and not beyond.

What happens if you are driving someone else's car or they are driving yours?

Many motorists are unclear about this but the law is specific: anyone driving a motor vehicle must be insured to drive *that* vehicle, either under their own policy or the vehicle owner's policy. If you are "comprehensively" covered, you will usually be insured to drive someone else's car with their consent; but for "third party only" cover, not for injury to yourself! Whatever your own insurance, you should always check that your use of another car is covered, preferably "comprehensively", by its owner's own policy.

Similarly, if letting someone else drive your car, you should make sure he is insured to drive it. If not, you are at risk of being prosecuted for permitting him to use the car while uninsured, which carries the same heavy penalties as if you were using it yourself without insurance.

Road Worthiness and the MOT

It is an offence for anyone, whether motor trader or private individual, to sell a motor vehicle "in an unroadworthy condition", and anyone who uses one on a road in a dangerous condition commits an offence against Section 40A of the 1988 Road Traffic Act. The sentence is a maximum £2,500 fine, endorsement with three points and discretionary disqualification. A fixed penalty is available, but only in less serious cases.

Few people use cars that are positively "dangerous" but many drivers may occasionally be in breach of the 1986 Motor Vehicle (Construction and Use) Regulations. These create a whole variety of maintenance offences, varying from inefficient brakes to having no water in a windscreen-washer bottle.

As we have already seen [see *Driving Licence*], the 1988 Act gives a uniformed police officer the right to stop at any time anyone driving a car on a road. If the officer chooses, he may then spot-check your vehicle's maintenance and, if he finds something wrong, he has three options. He can report you for prosecution, give you a fixed penalty notice or hand you a "vehicle defect form". This form will specify what is wrong and give you the opportunity of taking the car to an MOT garage to have it put right. If within 14 days you then produce the form, stamped by the garage, at a police station, that will be an end of it.

The three most serious offences under the 1986 Regulations carry a maximum £2,500 fine, endorsement with three points and discretionary disqualification. They relate to brakes, steering and tyres.

Brakes and steering are straightforward. Every part of the system must be in good working order and if a police officer finds, for instance, excessive travel on the brake pedal or play in the steering, however small, those are offences.

Tyre requirements are, however, more specific. Every tyre must have at least 1.6mm of tread in a continuous band all the way around the circumference and across 75 per cent of the tread, with *each* defective tyre counting as a separate offence. As for spare tyres: you do not legally have to carry one, but if you do, and use it, its tread must comply with the Regulations.

Most other offences — defective windscreen wipers, windscreens so dirty or cracked that you cannot properly see through them, broken mirrors, faulty exhaust, etc — attract a lesser maximum fine of £1,000 and no endorsement, penalty points or disqualification. As we have already seen, the fixed penalty system applies.

What about the MOT test certificate?

This was first introduced in the 1950s for cars more

than ten years old. But the age limit was progressively reduced and Section 47 of the 1988 Act now makes it an offence to use on a road any car older than three years without a current MOT (ie Ministry of Transport) certificate.

The certificate (scheduled to be replaced later in 1997 by a computerised entry on a national database) lasts for a year and, if caught without one, it can cost a maximum £1,000 fine. Magistrates used to impose comparatively low fines, but lately they have tended to treat this offence more seriously. Yet some experts still consider it under-punished with no endorsement, penalty points or even discretionary disqualification, although the fixed penalty system does not apply.

The 1981 Motor Vehicles (Test) Regulations specify what examiners must test, and it is a pretty long list: braking system, steering gear, lighting equipment and reflectors, stop lamps, tyres, seat belts, direction indicators, windscreen wipers and washers, exhaust system, audible warning instrument, body work and suspension.

The examination is detailed and rigorous. For instance, cars will fail if they have rusted or damaged bodywork with loose or ill-fitting bolts, rivets or welds and cracks or corrosion that affect body strength within 30cm of body mountings.

Our roads are dangerous enough without the extra hazard of mechanically unsafe vehicles.

ON THE ROAD

Seat Belts

Most people think that a seat belt is a seat belt and that both driver and front seat passengers, of whatever age, must wear one — and that's about it! In fact, the law is extremely complicated for such an everyday matter.

All cars manufactured since 1965 have to be produced with adult front seat belts, and all cars manufactured since 1987 must come with rear seat belts. That said, there are still some older cars legally on the road without front seat belts and even more without rear seat belts.

But it has been an offence ever since 1983, with certain exceptions (when reversing, anyone with a medical exemption certificate, taxi-drivers and mini-cab drivers, etc), for a driver and passenger aged 14 or over not to wear a fitted front seat belt, and since 1991 not to wear a fitted rear seat belt.

The fixed penalty system applies but the maximum courtroom fine for not wearing a seat belt under the 1993 Motor Vehicles (Wearing of Seat Belts) Regulations is £500. Who is liable? Drivers are responsible for themselves and children under 14. Otherwise, it is down to every adult passenger.

Not wearing a seat belt can also cost you dearly in a *civil* court, if suing for damages after an accident caused by another driver's negligence. Back in 1975, before seat belt wearing was even made compulsory, the Appeal Court ruled that it was obviously so sensible to belt up that not doing so should cut an adult person's damages because of their own "contributory negligence".

As Lord Denning laid down, if wearing a seat belt would have avoided all injury, an adult person's damages may be cut by 25 per cent — and by 15 per cent, if the injuries would have been "a good deal less severe".

What about children who, incidentally, are too young to be "contributorily negligent"?

Modern criminal law is extremely complicated. For instance, when my son was a baby, I used to put him in a carry-cot on the back seat but, if a police officer saw me doing that with my grandson, I could receive a fixed penalty notice or be fined. Nowadays the use of a carry-cot, on either a front or rear seat, is permitted *but only if the cot is strapped*. You must put the seat belt around it and fasten it. Otherwise you could be in trouble!

It is illegal nowadays to carry any unrestrained child in the front seat of a car. A child under three can only travel legally in a front seat, if an appropriate child restraint is worn. ("Appropriate child restraint" means a baby carrier, child seat, harness or booster seat appropriate to the child's weight, which will be clearly marked on the label.)

The Department of Transport advises that, if no child restraint is available for a child under three, it is generally safer for it to wear an adult belt alone, in the back seat, rather than no restraint at all.

Between three and 11, a "small child" (ie under 1.5 metres — about 5 feet — tall) can travel in front with a child restraint, if available. But if there is no child restraint in the front or back, nor an adult belt in the back, but an adult belt is fitted in the front, that is where the child must travel. The child *can* travel in the back but a child restraint or adult belt must be worn, if available.

Between 12 and 13 or with a "large child" under that age (ie 1.5 metres or taller), a child can sit in the front or back of a car; but an adult belt must be worn, if available.

I said that the subject was complex!

Speeding

This is the most frequently committed motoring offence. Most of us do it, though no doubt we like to think only "within reason". But there is *never* a legal excuse, except when driving a vehicle for fire brigade, ambulance or police purposes.

For the rest, when caught, we can only throw ourselves on the mercy of the police officer who has stopped us. A lot depends on the individual officer and on your own attitude. Politeness usually pays dividends.

However, it is useful to know that, under chief constables' "flexible" guidelines, if you exceed the limit by up to 10mph, you will probably get only a warning for future behaviour, and if you are between 10mph and 25mph over the limit, the officer will probably offer you a fixed penalty — which, as a general rule, you should accept. It will cost much less than going to court: £40 and three penalty points as against a fine of up to £1,000 (or £2,500, if speeding on a motorway), your licence endorsed and three to six penalty points.

Only if you have exceeded the relevant limit by more than 25mph, will you usually not be offered a fixed penalty and have to go to court.

What are the limits? Unless official signs show otherwise, they are 30mph on "restricted roads" (ie roads in built-up areas with street lights not more than 200 yards apart), 60mph on single carriageways, and 70mph on dual carriageways and motorways.

Incidentally, if you are towing a caravan or trailer, those last two limits are lowered by 10mph, which not everyone remembers!

Most people know that nowadays you can temporarily lose your licence for speeding, but when exactly is this likely to happen?

There is no "law" on the subject. The 1988 Road Traffic Offenders Act merely says that disqualification is "discretionary". So, in September 1993, the Magistrates' Association issued its own guidelines.

They are due to be updated later this year but, as of

the time of writing, magistrates are advised to "consider disqualification" if a motorist is 30mph over the relevant limit. So that someone travelling at over 60mph in a built-up area with a speed limit of 30mph is as likely to lose his or her licence for a short while as someone travelling at over 100mph on a motorway.

The guidelines continue:

30-34mph over the limit: six penalty points, £210 fine and seven days' ban;

35-39mph over the limit: six penalty points, £240 fine and 14 days' ban;

40mph or more over the limit: "a sharp increase" in both fine and ban, with a minimum of 21 days.

But do not forget that a motorist who persists in breaking the law may lose his licence for a minimum six months by a court "totting-up" his penalty points over the past three years, if that brings his total to 12 points or more — not necessarily all for speeding.

Being in Proper Control

You must give your whole attention to driving. Recently an off-duty policeman driving along the M4 was overtaken at 70mph by a man reading a book propped open on the steering wheel. He gave chase and the 25-year-old executive was banned for three months and fined £250 with £400 costs at Cardiff Crown Court after admitting dangerous driving.

That was an extreme case. Most drivers not giving their full attention to what they are doing breach a lesser offence, created by Regulation 104 of the 1986 Road Vehicles (Construction and Use) Regulations. This states that anyone "driving a motor vehicle on a road in such a position that he cannot have proper control of the vehicle" can be fined up to £1,000, although the fixed penalty system applies.

We have all been taught to concentrate on what we are doing and drive with both hands on the steering wheel. The many motorists who, for instance, choose to drive with only one hand firmly on the wheel and the other hand lightly touching it, with their arm resting casually on or outside the open window, are inviting a zealous police officer to stop and, at the very least, rebuke them.

My own two favourite Reg. 104 cases are the duke's daughter fined £75 for being locked in "a passionate embrace with her passenger" as she sped along the fast lane on the M6. And the judge on his way to Newcastle-upon-Tyne Crown Court who was pulled in and later given a written caution for steering with one hand and shaving with the other; at least he had the grace to admit, "It was a very silly thing to do."

What about mobile car phones? Do they fall foul of Reg. 104?

Many motorists believe that driving with only one hand on the wheel and the other holding a mobile phone is, in itself, perfectly legal and only becomes an offence if an accident were to occur through both hands not being on the wheel.

But there does not have to be an accident. Rare but successful prosecutions have occurred without.

In fact, if the police were fully to enforce Reg. 104, many more motorists who happily combine driving with talking on the phone would find themselves in court. As Rule 43 of the latest (1996) edition of the Highway Code rightly states: "You MUST exercise proper control of your vehicle at all times. Do not use a hand-held telephone or microphone while you are driving. Find a safe place to stop first."

(Incidentally, not many people know the exact legal status of the Highway Code. It does not create offences, in itself, but breach of its provisions can be used to prove that some other offence — such as, breach of Regulation 104 — has taken place.)

What about hands-free mobiles where the driver has both hands on the wheel?

They are almost certainly in a different legal category. It can be argued that motorists speaking on the phone, even when hands-free, are not giving their whole attention to their driving. That is why Rule 43 continues: "Do not speak into a hands-free microphone if it will take your mind off the road." But I do not know of a successful prosecution under Reg. 104 of a hands-free telephoning motorist, without any consequent accident.

Hands-free car phones are a legally safer, if more expensive, option.

Zebra Crossings

Once a pedestrian steps onto a "zebra", he has territorial immunity. Under the 1971 "Zebra" Crossing Regulations, you must "accord him precedence" if he has stepped onto the crossing before your vehicle has arrived there. You must stop and let him pass, even if he put his foot on to the black and white stripes when your front wheels were already on the zigzag approach area.

If not, you risk a fine of up to £1,000, three penalty points and (at least, in theory) a brief disqualification.

Fortunately, the soft option of a £40 fixed penalty may be available: usually if your speed was reasonable and the pedestrian gave you no chance to stop in time.

Each part of the crossing on either side of a central bollard counts as a separate zebra. But you still should be wary that they might continue across.

As a High Court judge said back in 1955: "It is the duty of any motorist approaching a zebra crossing to do so in such a way that he can deal with the situation when he gets there. He must be in a position, and driving at such a speed, that if anybody is on the crossing he is in a position to stop."

Beware of misreading the scene and thinking that a

pedestrian is letting you pass: "waiving his precedence", as lawyers call it. If you are mistaken and the pedestrian does not really mean it, you still commit an offence.

Zebra crossings can even get a motorist into trouble vis-à-vis other drivers. If you see another driver stopped to allow a pedestrian to cross, you cannot pass him — even if no one has yet stepped onto the crossing or they have already arrived on the opposite pavement.

The fact that another driver has stopped "for the purpose of complying with the Regulations" means that you also must do so, even unnecessarily.

Traffic Lights

For a start, what actually do they mean? Red alone is a legal command to "Stop", and you must wait behind the line marked on the road. Red and Amber also mean "Stop", and you must not pass through or start until Green shows. Amber alone means "Stop", and you may go on only if the light appears after you have crossed the stop line or are so close to it that to pull up might cause an accident.

Green means that you may go on, but only if the road is clear. It is not a command to continue. You should treat its invitation to proceed with caution. As the Highway Code advises, "Take special care if you intend to turn left or right and give way to pedestrians who are crossing."

And, of course, do not "jump the lights". That could lead not only to a charge of failing to obey traffic lights which carries a maximum fine of £1,000 and three penalty points, although the fixed penalty system applies, but also to the more serious charge of careless driving with a maximum fine of £2,500 and three to nine penalty points — with no fixed penalty.

Four common situations are of interest:

The traffic lights do not work

If you disobey an official set of traffic lights, whether working properly or not, you commit an offence against the 1994 Traffic Signs Regulations. But if the lights are jammed at red, you must either turn round and find another outlet or else stop — and remain stopped until a police officer or traffic warden comes along and countermands the red light by beckoning you forward.

However, a judge commented many years ago in a case at Hertford Quarter Sessions (the equivalent of a present-day Crown Court) that, if a motorist were to edge forward carefully without causing any damage or injury, the appropriate sentence would usually be only an absolute discharge; which almost does not count as a conviction. So, in practice, you would probably get only a mild rebuke.

But if the lights fail completely and show nothing, you can treat the junction as uncontrolled and commit no offence, even technically, in carefully proceeding.

Traffic lights at road works

What is their legal status? Some motorists believe that, even when they are showing red, you do not have to stop if you can safely see your way ahead. That is simply not so. The 1994 Regulations give portable temporary lights at road works and temporary road-traffic-control schemes equal validity with permanent traffic lights. If they show red, you must stop, even if the way ahead is clear.

Aggressive windscreen-cleaners at traffic lights

They are breaking the law. Section 5 of the 1986 Public Order Act clearly states: "Using threatening, abusive or insulting words or behaviour or disorderly behaviour in public within the hearing or sight of a person likely to be caused harassment, alarm or distress thereby" commits an offence for which they can be fined up to £1,000. The police, with other priorities in mind, tend to be reluctant to act; but that is another matter.

Need police cars, ambulances and fire engines obey traffic lights?

Not if it hinders their work. A Home Office spokesman explains: "There is no carte blanche for drivers of emergency service vehicles to disregard red traffic lights or any other road sign. However, the legislation encourages drivers on emergency journeys to regard red traffic lights as a 'Give Way' sign. Once they have alerted other drivers to their presence and indicated the direction they wish to take, they can pass through red lights *as soon as it is safe to do so.*"

What about a motorist giving way to police cars, etc? Is that courtesy or a legal obligation? There is no specific law which says you have to but, if you did not, you could be prosecuted for driving without reasonable consideration for other road users, a variant of careless driving.

Motorways (and hard shoulders)

Most of us know something about the special legal rules that apply to motorways: no learner-drivers, tractors, cyclists or moped riders, no picking up or setting down of passengers, etc.

The fixed penalty system applies but three situations may cause particular problems:

Leaving the motorway

Do not, like so many motorists, suddenly pull out of an overtaking lane in front of drivers in the nearside left-hand lane, who then may have to brake sharply. If a police patrol were to see it, you could be warned about inconsiderate driving.

Similarly, if pulling on to the hard shoulder in an emergency or when directed by official traffic signs or the police, you should, even if already in the left-hand lane, try not to move abruptly onto the shoulder but first slow down so that traffic behind is not inconvenienced.

What is an emergency entitling you to pull onto the hard shoulder?

Regulation 7 of the 1982 Motorways Traffic (England and Wales) Regulations says that you can stop on a hard shoulder "by reason of any accident, illness or other emergency" but — of course! — does not say what constitutes an emergency.

Fortunately, Lord Widgery, when Lord Chief Justice, has ruled exactly what "emergency" means. It was in a case where a tired motorist had pulled onto the hard shoulder because he thought that it was no longer safe to continue driving.

Basing himself on the dictionary definition of emergency as "a sudden and/or unexpected occurrence", Lord Widgery said: "Too much stress must not be attached to the word 'sudden'." The tiredness does not have to attack the motorist at the very second before he pulls onto the hard shoulder. "If he gets onto the carriageway at a time when, so far as he could see, it was safe and lawful for him to proceed to the next turn-off point, it is sufficient to show that something intervened which rendered it unsafe to proceed to that next turn-off point."

An urgent call of nature making it impossible to concentrate properly on driving *could* be an emergency, but you would have to persuade a police officer —

perhaps eventually a court — that you had had no prior warning before you passed the last exit.

Can you lawfully make a U-turn on the motorway to go back the other way and avoid a long traffic jam ahead?

You risk a fine of up to £2,500, your licence endorsed with three penalty points and discretionary disqualification for breach of Regulation 10 of the 1982 Regulations. It could even amount to careless or dangerous driving.

But if it merely means taking advantage of a convenient gap in the central reservation, *and you are careful*, you may consider it worth the risk. You will still be fined, but you may avoid penalty points.

In a 1988 case where a motorist on the M23 had driven through a gap and started to drive back along the other carriageway after an accident had caused a major traffic jam ahead, the High Court ruled that local magistrates had been right not to endorse his licence.

Said Mr Justice French: "If the motorway had been in normal use, it would have been difficult, perhaps impossible, for the justices to have found 'special reasons' not to endorse.

"However, the motorway was plainly not in normal use. The defendant did not have to halt before executing his U-turn. He was already at a halt. He had ample opportunity to study the carriageway into which he was about to turn."

Those last words are vital. The driver had not cut across oncoming traffic. He had carefully assessed the situation. Even so, I do not recommend any such manoeuvre.

Careless and Dangerous Driving

Until recently, even lawyers like myself were not entirely sure if they knew the answer to the question: What is the difference between careless and dangerous driving?

A fixed penalty is not available and the difference in punishment is very substantial.

Dangerous driving carries up to two years' imprisonment and/or an unlimited fine with obligatory disqualification (one year for a first offence and three years for a second offence within three years) or endorsement with three to 11 penalty points, if no special reasons exist. Furthermore, if a court disqualifies, you will not get your licence back after the disqualification until you have taken — and passed — a new "extended" driving test which is about twice as long as the original L-driver's test.

On the other hand, careless driving carries no possibility of prison and has a maximum fine of £2,500, with *discretionary* disqualification and endorsement with only three to nine penalty points in the absence of special reasons.

But Parliament never specified how bad the quality of driving must be to differentiate the lesser offence from the other. Section 2A of the 1988 Road Traffic Act merely states: "A person is to be regarded as driving dangerously if, and only if, (a) the way he drives falls below [that vague phrase is nowhere defined] what would be expected of a competent and careful driver and (b) it would be obvious to a competent and careful driver that driving in that way would be dangerous." In other words, dangerous means dangerous. Not terribly helpful.

As for careless driving, Section 3 of the 1988 Act creates two versions of the same offence: "driving without due care and attention" and "driving without reasonable consideration for other persons using the road." This latter is more properly known, not as "careless driving" but "inconsiderate driving". And the prosecuting authorities cannot charge both careless and inconsiderate driving. They must choose which one to go for.

The result of this sloppy draftsmanship was that for many years the police, lawyers and even magistrates were sometimes unsure about the exact difference between the two offences, except for the vague notion that one was more serious than the other.

However, last year the Crown Prosecution Service published official guidance which has very much helped police and prosecutors to know which offence to charge in any particular case.

Largely unknown to the general motoring public, it gives valuable specific examples. Hence: careless driving is stated to be acts of driving caused by more than momentary inattention in which road users' safety is affected, such as overtaking on the inside, driving inappropriately close to another vehicle or driving through a red light. It is also conduct that clearly caused the driver not to be in a position to respond to an emergency, such as using a hand-held mobile phone when the vehicle is moving (especially when at speed), tuning a car radio or reading a newspaper or map.

Inconsiderate driving is instanced as: flashing lights to force other drivers in front to give way; misuse of any lane to avoid queuing or gain some other advantage over other drivers; unnecessarily remaining in an overtaking lane or unnecessarily slow driving or braking without good cause.

What about dangerous driving? Examples are given as: racing or competitive driving; highly inappropriate speed for prevailing road or traffic conditions; aggressive or intimidatory driving, such as sudden lane changes, cutting into a line of vehicles or driving too close to the vehicle in front, especially when intended to cause the other vehicle to pull to one side to allow the accused to overtake; deliberate disregard of traffic lights or other roads signs; and prolonged, persistent or deliberate bad driving.

All that makes very good sense. But why did we have to wait so long to know the answer?

(The concept of dangerous driving does not apply in civil law. There the issue is not whether anyone shall go to gaol or be fined, but whether the motorist at fault [or more often his insurance company] will have to pay compensation to any victim. The sole question is whether the motorist has been guilty of *negligent* driving — which is very similar to careless driving. This is failing to take reasonable care in all the circumstances, which means exactly what it says: there are no preconceptions, such as the common erroneous belief that in an accident the car behind is always legally to blame.)

Road Rage

As a legal concept, "road rage" does not exist. The loss of temper, however violent, by a motorist involved in a driving incident is not an offence in itself. It can be an ingredient in several other offences which can vary from a minor breach of the peace or public order offence, such as a rude gesture or offensive remark while at the wheel (which will seldom get to court), to dangerous driving, serious assault or even, in mercifully rare cases, murder.

Most people believe it is strictly a modern phenomenon. The term has been current in Britain for only about the past two years, and is said to have been first used in April 1988 in the United States when a Florida newspaper reported that in a local court case, "a fit of road rage has landed a man in jail."

In fact, of course, drivers have been losing their tempers with each other ever since the first motor cars trundled onto the roads. Yet it is undoubtedly true that only comparatively recently have there been so many cases.

At first, the courts were slow to respond. They tended only to impose a fine and penalty points or perhaps a short disqualification. But from about early last year motorists who had never before seen the inside of a prison have begun to find themselves tasting the experience.

And not only men. As London stipendiary magistrate Mrs Ros Keating said in September 1996: "Any kind of assault when someone is enraged on the road must result in prison. It happens far too often these days." That was when a 49-year-old businesswoman — presumably not usually a female thug — had attacked a 30-year-old woman journalist after a minor traffic incident in the respectable London area of Chelsea. She pulled her victim's hair, smacked her head against her car bonnet, then bit her above her right eyebrow. She was jailed for 30 days.

In the previous month, when jailing a 69-year-old pensioner for 18 months for pulling a folding knife and stabbing a 45-year-old motorist in a row about the older man's driving, Judge John Swanson said at Leeds Crown Court: "Violence arising from disputes between motorists in cars will normally result in a prison sentence. When the facts are accompanied by a weapon, the sentence must be substantial." And it made no difference that the victim had brought the attack upon himself by chasing the pensioner to a car park because he thought that he had cut him up on the road.

In January 1997, in the first "road rage" case to reach the Appeal Court, Lord Bingham, the present Lord Chief Justice, gave a lead to all other judges by increasing from six months to two years the prison sentence on a 27-year-old Manchester motorist who had seriously injured another driver and his passenger in a totally unjustified attack. "The courts should be seen to punish such conduct severely," said Lord Bingham.

Killing Someone

Even the best driver can find himself in this dire plight. With thousands of people killed every year on our roads, this is sadly a question of practical interest to everyone who drives.

The penalty, if any, depends upon the specific motoring offence committed. Victims' sorrowing relatives may not agree but judges are continually saying, and most motorists would say rightly, that you cannot argue backwards from the consequences of a particular piece of driving and say: "Somebody was killed. So the level of bad driving must necessarily have been the worst."

Any experienced motoring lawyer knows that a person can be killed on the roads without a driver being legally — or even morally — to blame. Some accidents just happen, while others are quite honestly the victim's own fault. And even if a motorist is to blame, it may be merely momentary inattention or an atypical error of judgement by someone with a good driving record.

So what are the major offences with which a driver involved in a fatal road accident may be faced?

Manslaughter

This is the most serious, but also the rarest. It carries a maximum penalty of life imprisonment and is usually reserved for joy-riding adults who drive with no concern for their own or anyone else's safety.

Causing death by careless driving while under the influence of drink or drugs or with excess alcohol in the body

The 1991 Road Traffic Act created this offence with disqualification (and a new "extended" driving test), except for "special reasons", and a maximum five years in prison — quickly increased to ten years by the 1993 Criminal Justice Act. Appeal Court decisions have since indicated that the average sentence should be around the old maximum of five years.

Causing death through dangerous driving

The 1991 Act also created this new offence with disqualification (and a new "extended" driving test), except for "special reasons", and a maximum five years in prison, similarly increased to ten years by the 1993 Act. This is the offence with which a normally careful motorist with a good driving record is most likely to be charged.

Sentences vary from six months to four years, depending on the circumstances. For instance, a 54-year-old retired millionaire businessman who killed two pensioners when he crashed into their car when showing off his wife's £130,000 Ferrari at high speed, was jailed for nine months. He was banned from driving for seven years and Judge David Wilcox told him at Shrewsbury Crown Court that the public would have been "outraged" if he had not sent him to gaol, even though he had suffered severe depression since the crash.

At the lowest level of culpability, one can be charged just with careless driving, carrying only a maximum fine of £2,500 with no risk of jail and only discretionary disqualification (ie even without "special reasons").

A typical case was a 37-year-old man who lost control of his car when travelling at high speed over a humpback bridge in Cleveland. He collided head-on with an oncoming vehicle, killing its driver and his own two young women passengers. In January 1996, Teesside magistrates fined him £1,500 and banned him from driving for six months. The victims' relatives shouted their disbelief as the punishment was announced.

Is all this fair? I ask you to consider these words of Lord Taylor, then Lord Chief Justice, in December 1993: "We wish to stress that human life cannot be restored nor even its loss measured by the length of a prison sentence. We recognise that no term of months or years imposed on the offender can reconcile the family of a deceased victim to their loss, nor will it cure their anguish." And, I would add, lessen the long-lasting sense of guilt of any decent motorist.

Drink-driving

The modern law is contained in the 1988 Road Traffic Act. Forget all those weird defences about offering the penis or other sensitive parts of the body for a blood test, or downing a swig of whisky so that the police cannot get an accurate alcohol reading. They have all gone.

The motorist who drinks and drives today faces, if caught, almost certain disqualification for at least 12 months, a maximum £5,000 fine and, in a really bad case, up to six months in prison.

Let me spell out as precisely as I can the somewhat complex legal position.

Anyone driving or attempting to drive a motor vehicle on a road or any other public place — which can include a public house car park — commits an offence if he has more than 35 microgrammes (mcg) of alcohol in 100 millilitres (ml) of his breath, 80 milligrammes (mlg) of alcohol in 100ml of his blood, or 107mlg of alcohol in 100ml of his urine.

A uniformed police officer — not one in plain clothes — can stop you and ask you to take a breath test at the roadside if he reasonably suspects you of having alcohol in your body, even though he does not think you are over the limit.

He can also stop you if you have committed a moving traffic offence, however slight, or if you have had an accident. Indeed, most forces, including Scotland Yard, now have a policy of breath-testing every driver involved in an accident, even the innocent party.

That is not all. Although few forces would admit to doing it, random breath-testing is lawful. Lord Widgery, when Lord Chief Justice, ruled as far back as 1972 that a uniformed police officer can stop a motorist at any time; so if he then smells alcohol on the driver's breath, he can ask for the test. His actual words were: "The mere fact that a check can be described as random is no grounds for dismissing a drink-driving charge." Simple!

What if you manage to get back home ahead of the police?

Many drivers think that gives them sanctuary, but that is not necessarily so.

If you have had an accident in which someone else has been hurt, a uniformed officer can enter your home by force, if necessary, and request a breath test. All other cases constitute a grey area. A motorist may be acquitted, even if over the limit, if a court later rules that the police have been guilty of what Lord Woolf once called "oppressive behaviour": such as, pushing their way into one's home and claiming to have rights which they know they do not have.

What happens if you refuse a roadside breath test?

Doing so without reasonable excuse is, in itself, an offence carrying a maximum £1,000 fine, four penalty points and discretionary disqualification. You will be arrested and taken to a police station where the usual procedure will follow. You have only chalked up more trouble.

At the police station, if the roadside breath test has proved positive or you have been arrested for not giving one, you will be asked for a specimen of breath sufficient for instant analysis by an electronic device. Several approved devices exist but the Camic and Lion Intoximeters are most popular. You cannot ask to wait until your solicitor arrives.

You must give two specimens and the print-out is immediate, although, in fairness, only the lower reading is used.

To allow for machine error, the police will drop the matter if the lower reading is between 35 and 40mcg. And there is a further safeguard: if the reading does not exceed 50mcg, or the station has no electronic device, the police *must* offer you an alternative test of blood or urine, although they choose which one! Blood can only be taken by a doctor and the police must ask if there is any medical reason against it. When a constable ignored a driver's reply, "I'm taking tablets", the subsequent conviction was overturned on appeal because the constable should have asked more questions.

The only "reasonable excuse" for not giving blood or urine is if you are physically or mentally unable to do so, or it would entail a substantial risk to your health; either of which you would later have to prove in court.

Nowadays, defence lawyers tend not to waste their energies on trying to get their clients off completely. They concentrate on trying to argue that, although there must be a fine, "special reasons" exist for not disqualifying.

In rare cases, this can be done. For instance: if the motorist only drove because of a sudden medical emergency and no other transportation was available, or someone had laced his drink without his knowing it and he would otherwise have been within the limit.

But it is absolutely useless to try and say that you were only just over the limit, or your driving was not impaired, or your livelihood will suffer, or you were drinking only a comparatively small amount on an empty stomach.

You should have thought of all that before you had a drink — and, needless to say, a fixed penalty is not available.

Accidents

What to do if you have an accident? This is possibly the most misunderstood aspect of everyday motoring law.

Section 170 of the 1988 Road Traffic Act gives the answer. Your first duty is to stop. Obviously you should use common sense and, if possible, not stop in the middle of a busy road but try to pull in to the kerb.

If another motorist is involved, he also must stop; but do not let him intimidate you into calling the police. They will usually only come if someone has been injured. Your only obligation is, "if required by any person having reasonable grounds to do so" (eg the other driver or the owner of damaged property), to give your name and address, those of the car's owner if it is not yours, and its index number — as well as your insurance certificate if someone is injured. Of course, this applies vice-versa to any other motorist involved.

Many drivers think they can automatically demand driving licence and insurance certificate; but Section 170 says nothing about a driving licence and states that a motorist only has to show his insurance certificate in case of injury.

But not every accident means that you must stop and give particulars. That only applies when someone besides yourself is hurt, when property or another vehicle is damaged, or when a horse, ass, mule, sheep, pig, goat, dog or cattle not in your own vehicle are injured. But not a cat!

If you do not give particulars at the time, perhaps because no one else was there (as with the absent owner of a damaged parked car), it is no defence to say that no one was around. You must report the accident at a police station or to a police officer "as soon as reasonably practicable and in any case within 24 hours."

Those words mean what they say. You cannot cavalierly put off reporting for up to 24 hours. You must do it as soon as reasonably practicable. Only if you cannot, do you have up to 24 hours in which to do so.

Furthermore, the High Court has ruled that you cannot simply telephone a police station to report. You must do it in person. Failure to stop and failure to report to the police are two separate offences. A fixed penalty is *not* available and you could, if unlucky (or stupid), find yourself convicted of both offences — each carrying a maximum six months' jail sentence and/or £5,000 fine, five to ten penalty points and discretionary disqualification.

The only exception is if you can persuade a Bench of cynical magistrates that you genuinely did not know there had been an accident. This is unlikely with an accident on the open road but, when trying to manoeuvre in or out of tightly parked cars, it is not entirely impossible. Some years ago, the Queen's cousin Lord Harewood was acquitted at Bow Street magistrates' court in Central London when he successfully claimed that he had not realised he had backed into a parked car because he was listening to a Mozart wind serenade on his car radio. He explained that he might have confused the sound of a burglar alarm, set off on the parked car, with a sustained note on the clarinet.

One final point: Because a cat is not an "animal" within Section 170, do not callously think it is safe to drive on. If you could reasonably help the stricken creature, you should stop; otherwise, if anyone saw you, they could report you for causing it unnecessary suffering, contrary to the 1911 Protection of Animals Act — which does define a cat as an "animal".

Parking

"No Waiting" restrictions are a fact of modern life. Yellow lines on the road mean that parking there — technically, "waiting" — is illegal at all times or within restricted hours on weekdays and sometimes also on Sunday, with the restrictions greater on double than single yellow lines.

What are those restrictions?

With double yellow lines, they can extend for 24 hours a day, seven days a week. They vary greatly and motorists often genuinely do not know where they can legally park and for how long.

The only answer is to look at notices displayed at the entry to every controlled parking zone. These must state the restricted times, in general, for that zone; but if, as sometimes happens, they are different in certain streets, there must also be small official plates by the kerb *in those very streets* giving the precise details. As the Highway Code states: "Yellow lines can only give a guide to the restrictions in force, and time plates or zone entry signs must be consulted."

But drivers also want to pick up and drop off passengers or load and unload goods: how does that work?

Except on London's new-style red routes, which we shall look at in a moment, you can always *briefly* pick up or drop off passengers; but the situation with loading is more complicated. Loading is permitted on yellow lines during restricted hours, except where there is a specific loading ban, which will be shown by one or by two yellow stripes on the kerb as well as on the road itself. The actual times of the loading ban are always shown on a white sign by the kerb.

But be careful. Stopping for permitted loading or unloading is not the same as stopping for quick shopping. The goods must be of a type that cannot easily be carried to the vehicle by one person in one trip. "They cannot be a fountain pen," as a High Court judge once commented.

Within restricted hours in controlled parking zones, where can you lawfully park?

The answer is only on a parking meter, in a Pay &

Display area or, if you hold a local resident's permit, on a residential parking bay. (Unless official plates warn otherwise, non-residents can park on residential parking bays outside restricted hours.) With parking meters and Pay & Display areas, you must buy on arrival all the time you want (usually up to two hours), with no time allowed for finding change, and you cannot later "feed" the meter or buy a second display voucher. You also cannot park on a meter showing "OUT OF ORDER" or covered by an official "No Parking" bag.

On some major roads in London, yellow lines have been replaced by red lines. These are the new "red routes" which, at times stated on warning plates by the roadside, ban *all* stopping — for whatever purpose.

If you or your passenger is disabled with a card displaying an official Orange Badge issued by the local council, except for loading prohibitions, yellow lines do not apply and there are exemptions from other parking restrictions.

Apart from all these restrictions, it is also an offence to "leave a motor vehicle in a dangerous position" (maximum £1,000 fine, three penalty points and discretionary — but rare — disqualification) and to "cause or permit an unnecessary obstruction" (maximum £1,000 fine alone). The fixed penalty system applies to both.

Since July 1994, most illegal parking in London has been "decriminalised" and is no longer dealt with by police officers or traffic wardens. Save for obstruction, parking on zigzag lines or red routes, law enforcement has been handed over to uniformed parking attendants employed by the 33 London borough councils. A similar system may eventually spread elsewhere but so far only Winchester and Oxford have followed suit.

Under this new scheme, the old fixed penalty system does not apply. You either pay direct to the local council a penalty charge (no longer called a fine) which, according to the circumstances, can be £60, £40 or £20, and earn a 50 per cent discount by paying it within 14 days. Or if the full amount is still unpaid within another 14 days, the council claims for it, as a civil debt, in a county court.

If you believe that a parking attendant has wrongly or even unfairly given you a parking ticket (now called a penalty charge notice), you can write to the local council arguing that it should be withdrawn. From personal experience, I know that this sometimes succeeds. But if the council reject your plea, they must send you a form explaining that you can appeal to a panel of independent adjudicators. This is a free and informal service available either in person or through the post.

Successful cases include a pregnant mother who could not walk far and had vainly searched for a legitimate parking place, and an elderly man with a prostate problem who had to park illegally to visit urgently a public convenience.

These adjudicators have more leeway than magistrates had in the old days; but you must make the effort.

Towing Away and Clamping

A fine or penalty charge are, of course, not the only possible consequences of illegal parking. There are also the twin curses of a modern motorist's life: towing away and — so far only in London — on-road clamping. Besides the inconvenience, towing away costs a £105 release fee plus £12 a day storage, if you do not collect your car from the pound on the same day, *and* the parking fine or penalty charge. On-road clamping costs a £38 declamping fee plus the penalty charge.

Section 99 of the 1984 Road Traffic Regulation Act gives general authority for cars to be towed away when "illegally, obstructively or dangerously parked". For most police authorities the key words are "obstructively or dangerously", since to tow away every illegally parked vehicle would clearly be unrealistic. That said, many motorists would agree that cars merely parked illegally are often towed away.

In London and other parts of the country, the actual towing away is done by private firms operating at a profit. Although they need the prior authority of a police officer, traffic warden or parking attendant, some people suspect that their role may sometimes perhaps have as much to do with money-earning as with law enforcement.

As for clamping, there are two kinds: the on-road official version, limited only to London, and private off-road clamping which occurs throughout England and

Wales. This is when your car is parked without permission on private land and a release fee is demanded by the landowner or his contractor.

Contrary to popular belief, on-road clamping is not restricted to vehicles parked dangerously or for a long time. Like many other motorists in London, I have seen Post Office vehicles, delivery vans and even taxis clamped. In one case, a man's car was clamped while he was asleep inside!

The legal basis is that the 1984 Road Traffic Regulations Act enables a police officer or traffic warden to authorise on-road clamping when *any* parking law is infringed. London parking attendants have an even freer hand: the only legal restraint imposed by the 1991 Road Traffic Act is that vehicles on a meter cannot be clamped unless they have overstayed for at least 15 minutes!

What about private sector clamping on private property?

That presents its own problems. Outlawed in Scotland since July 1992 by a Court of Session ruling that it amounts to "extortion and theft", in England and Wales it flourishes. It is legal whenever you park on private land without permission *and a prominently displayed notice warns that you may be clamped and specifies the release fee.* As the Appeal Court ruled in November 1995, you are presumed to have read the notice and to have accepted its consequences.

However, Lord Bingham, then Master of the Rolls, said that the release fee must not be "unreasonable or exorbitant" and that there must be no delay in releasing the vehicle after the motorist has offered to pay.

Yet one still reads of "cowboy clampers" who reduce pregnant women to tears, take wedding rings and other jewellery as payment or hold children hostage while parents dash to get cash from banks.

The Government promised back in July 1992 that it was "urgently considering" what proposals to put before Parliament to curb such disgraceful practices. But despite strenuous representations by the motoring organisations, nothing has yet been forthcoming.

Driving Overseas

Obviously, local laws apply — and the drink-driving limit is often lower than in Britain! But here are some basic rules for taking your car to mainland Europe. If in doubt, check with the national tourist office or with a motoring organisation.

● Displaying a GB sticker is a legal requirement and you may be fined on the spot for not having one.

● Always take your driving licence and vehicle registration document. But a full UK driving licence is not always enough by itself. Italy and Austria require official translations and, in France and Portugal, drivers with a full licence for less than two years or one year respectively must observe special speed limits.

● It is generally an offence not to adjust your headlights for driving on the other side of the road. You can readily purchase beam converters at Channel ports and the Eurotunnel entrance.

● In many European countries, you must carry a first aid kit and a warning triangle for an accident or emergency.

● Third party cover is a minimum legal requirement throughout the European Union. Technically, you may not need a Green Card but I always ask my insurance broker for one — and immediately sign it. French entry police sometimes demand to see one and it can smooth your passage with local police in the event of an accident. Similarly, although not a legal necessity, you should always get a bail bond before visiting Spain; it can save you from being thrown into prison if you inadvertently injure someone!

LEGAL CONSEQUENCES

Going to Court

After defending many motorists, I can only report that you should, as a general rule, plead guilty and not fight a driving case in court unless (a) you have a burning sense of injustice (sadly, not always an infallible guide to courtroom success), (b) a competent lawyer advises that you have a good defence in law and (c), either way, you can afford it — going to court does not come cheap.

It is not enough to say: "I shall tell the truth on oath. They must believe me!" It does not always work out like that. Some years ago, a bishop contested a speeding summons and was astonished that the Bench accepted a policeman's word, "corroborated" by what he said was the reading on his motorcycle's speedometer, as against his own testimony in the witness box. "I am staggered that they accepted the policeman's evidence and not mine," he afterwards told a reporter. He even threatened to resign.

With motoring cases, you never can tell. I have won cases that I thought I would lose and lost many more that I thought I had a reasonable chance of winning. It is almost — but not quite — a lottery.

Most motoring offences not dealt with by the fixed penalty system can be dealt with by post and, if you plead guilty, a short courteous letter expressing your regret, stating such mitigation as may be available and apologising to the court, can do no harm.

Otherwise, even if pleading guilty, you may sometimes still have to go to court to give your side of things. This applies if the court is considering the possibility of disqualification (*which it must tell you in advance*) or if you want to argue that "special reasons" exist not to endorse your licence. Then, if you can possibly afford it, you should engage a lawyer to speak for you and, if necessary, take you through your story in the witness box. But ask your solicitor to find an experienced local barrister or solicitor-advocate who knows that particular Bench.

In all other cases, grab the chance of a fixed penalty notice, if offered!

Retaking the Driving Test

No one does this voluntarily and we have already seen that, when disqualifying for dangerous driving or causing death through dangerous driving, a court will order the defendant to take an extended driving test at the end of the disqualification.

There are also two other instances when a court can

order a defendant to be disqualified until he or she retakes their ordinary driving test. One is long-standing, the other is totally new:

(i) Section 36 of the 1988 Road Traffic Offenders Act, re-enacting earlier legislation, gives courts the power, with all endorsable offences, to re-order a driving test when necessary for "the safety of road users". Yet, as Mr Justice Talbot ruled back in 1975: "This is not a punitive power but should be used in respect of people who are growing old or infirm or show some incompetence in the offence which requires looking into."

Undoubtedly, this will often involve elderly people whose ability to drive safely has been brought into question, but it can include unsafe or arrogant drivers of whatever age.

(ii) The 1995 Road Traffic (New Drivers) Act, due to come into force in June 1997, states that drivers who notch up six penalty points within two years of passing their driving test will have to take it again. According to the Department of Transport, new drivers are twice as likely to have an accident as other motorists. "This should make roads safer for all," says the junior transport minister.

Motoring law not only punishes, it also protects.

Avoid the holiday breakdown blues!

There's no sadder sight than holiday makers stranded by the roadside because their car has broken down. Here are a few simple checks from the **Duckhams Helpline** to keep your holiday motoring on the road.

- Check the engine oil and top up as necessary with the correct grade.
- Check tyre pressures against those recommended in the car's handbook. A heavily laden car, or one travelling at continual high speeds, may well need higher pressure than normal. And remember to check the spare too!
- Top up the washer reservoir with water and a proprietory screenwash additive.
- Test all lights, including the brake lights.
- Check that the engine coolant is at the recommended level. For radiators with filler caps, it should be within 2cm of the filler neck.
- Top up the battery with distilled water, if required (though most modern cars now have "sealed for life" batteries).
- Check the brake fluid level — use only fresh fluid from a sealed container to top up.
- If you're towing a caravan or trailer, remember to check its lights and tyre pressures too.

And finally, although a car may use only a little oil for local driving, it can use a great deal more during lengthy high-speed motoring. A low level can result in overheating, excessive engine wear or even complete seizure. So check the level while you're away, and top up as necessary. For more information call the **Duckhams Helpline** on 0181 290 8207.

Happy holidays!